This

MW00938705

by KAITLYN N. LENTULO

Copyright © 2017 Kaitlyn N. Lentulo

All rights reserved.

ISBN-13: 978-1979183604
ISBN-10: 1979183600

About the book -

This poetry and prose collection is titled *This is for you* because my hope is that these words will be as freeing for you as they are for me. Written words relieve something within; they liberate thoughts from captivity. These pieces are not meant to stay safe and protected in stacks of journals. They can only do so much good there, and I've come to believe that they aren't only meant for me. My struggles are not only mine. My pain is not only mine. And my joys and stories of redemption should certainly not only be mine.

You are not alone. You have the power to rise above, to rise higher, to be a light in a place that needs it. You are enough. You are doing enough. You are human, and you are loved. In this world, we can expect to feel pain, to experience heartache and unwanted chaos, but we were built to last. We were built to endure and exude joy in the most brutally painful places. A silly family motto that I grew up with is, "We're not graceful, but we're sturdy." It's meant as an endearing joke, but there's actually substance there. Join me, as we walk through heartbreak, deep love, and some of life's greatest joys and sorrows together.

I hope you find rest here.

CONTENTS

Chapter 1: Erasing love.

To begin,
we will walk through the depths,
the darkness,
the pain and heartache
of broken relationship.

But please do not forget,
even as we enter the murkiest waters,
that there is hope
waiting for us at the surface.

I believe it to be no coincidence
that poetry is so often the product of pain.

I gently laid my trust in your open hands,
not knowing they were lined with dust,
a filth that still, to this day,
I have not been able to scrub away.

Will you forgive me if I run?
I was not prepared
for you to be here.
You showed up without notice,
and now I feel like the weight strung to my lungs,
dropped,
and is keeping me from inhaling
deeply enough
to stay alive.

I suppose the most dangerous thing about him
was that he could protect her
better than she could.

And she was now unsure
what use she was to herself.
Could he protect her from that?

THIS IS FOR YOU.

The light in his eyes grew dimmer over time.
I suppose all things eventually lose their shine.

THIS IS FOR YOU.

You live inside my airway,
controlling every breath I take,
telling me if I'm allowed to take the next.

I'm afraid I'll only be a wisp of smoke
when you return.
I burned for you every night and day.
You should have put me out
before you went away.

You must realize you're making people suffer,
by letting self-pity be your everyday lover.

It wasn't the way you looked at me
that made me want you more.

It was the way that you did not.

You like to take your time.
But the thing is, the time you took
was my time also.
You stole from me
something that cannot be replaced.

So in return,
my love for you
is permanently misplaced.

You will not steal another second
of my good grace.

The way you reach for me,
I cannot tell,
whether you are trying to lift me up
or push me down to hell.

Your words
strangled my self-esteem,
until I was brought all the way down
   onto my knees.

THIS IS FOR YOU.

To love me forever -

How self-obsessed you must be,
to forget you ever made
such a promise to me.

There was a fear in her.
But it wasn't of him.
It was of what she would do
    if she knew where he'd been.

He was like a good book.
She got lost in him
and forgot there would be an end.

I hope it goes well for you,
whatever it is you left me to do.

I figured you found someone else,
by the way you looked at me with no remorse.

And suddenly I feel responsible,
how much does that poor girl know?
I hope she knows enough
to leave while she's still whole.

All this to say,
I love a stranger more than I love you.

I hope you remember me,
when the air gets warmer
and the cool breeze disappears.

I hope you'll remember that we spent more time laughing
than we did crying
and that our love wasn't meant to stay cold forever.

She butchered his heart,
and from then on,
he only knew how to give it away in pieces.

Don't flatter yourself.
If you made her feel pain,
 she wasn't inspired by you.
She was made tired by you,
 and this is how she heals.
She was inspired by her own reaction,
 not by your distraction.

Stop holding onto me if I am only your life vest.
My dear, I love you.
But you will never learn to swim.

She wasn't sure if the goosebumps along her spine arose
because he made her feel cold
or because she was enticed.

Perhaps it was both.

We were too the same
in the sense that we both decided to leave,
when we had the choice to stay.

She didn't reach out to him
because she feared there would be nothing left
for him to hold in return.
She knew she had diminished herself.
She knew she was barely alive.
But she feared more,
that if she didn't reach out,
she would forever wish that she had tried.

When he hurts a friend -

Drop your chivalrous act, false gentleman.
You ruined your chance long before I met you.

Her fingers dripped of mercy,
her face, a gaze of grace.

But her touch was filled with fire.
Her words,
whipped with bitter distaste.

Heartbreak is a deep wound.
Slowly, it scabs over,
giving way to a new type of discomfort.

It is tempting to get rid of the scab,
often seeming ready to come off,
when it isn't.

How uncomfortable it is,
to see that you are healing
but to discover that you are still raw.

Once left alone,
the wound will become a story-filled scar.
Healed.

But here I struggle,
because even scars demand the eye's attention.

I wish you were as gone from my thoughts
as you are from my life.

To love you or leave you,
sometimes it's the same.

She pleaded with him to give back
whatever was left of her heart.
There had to be spare change.
She must've given him too much.
He looked at her and said,
"That was the price.
What you gave me is already spent."

I will not offer you my hand.
Steal it from me,
and pull me far from the ledge.

I want to tell him that he has my whole heart,
that his smile makes me swell,
and his absence makes me ache.
But pride intervenes and says,
"No. That will make you weak."

If your heart is broken,
remember that the pieces are still there.
They are going nowhere.
Give yourself time
to sort through them.

If only her standards were as high as her cheekbones.

Don't worry about him leaving.
You know the good ones stay.
And that's the only kind you want, anyway.

She missed knowing
    that even one person
loved her more deeply
than anyone else.

He looked at her and said,
"My love for you washes over me like waves,
but darling,
I don't want the waves.

I want something
that stays."

This is not love,
this thirst for more,
this greed.
This is lust.
This is perverse.
This is what burns me at the core.

I ran from you my whole youth.
I ran from you because you destroy.
You leave ruined,
you promise healing,
then you break.

Leave me be,
so I can find a love
    that does not depend on your drug.

What his father forgot -

As a child he remembered hearing,
"Let boys be boys
and girls be girls."

And that would've been ok,
if only his father had remembered to say,

"Women are feminine,
and men should be gentlemen."

I cringed at the thought of your hand on my back.
You were the last thing I wanted
invading my skin.

Are you sure you want me to leave,
when all you will have left
is your lock and my key?
It will never work this way, my love.
Please,
trust me.

If he is only soft with you
when you are crying,
    he is not soft at all.

I never stopped living when you left.
So do not come back
thinking you will resurrect something dead in me.

And one morning,
I woke up,
and did not miss you anymore.

As if I wouldn't feel a thing,
    if you walked right through the door.

Fight for me,
but do it peacefully.
If you leave any marks
it will only let the past seep in.

Please, speak freely.

I am not afraid of the words you will say to me;
I am afraid of the words you will not.

I've heard many answers to many questions about you.
And I am painfully
unsatisfied.

Oh darling,
    he didn't save you.
He just came into your life
right when you started saving yourself.

Chapter 2: Part I - Love in permanent ink.

She handed him her heart
and said,

"This is for you."

When she saw him,
her legs were outpaced
    by the racing of her heart.

I wasn't much for romance
until you taught me how to dance,
under the stars,
against the city lights.

You didn't try to kiss me.
The only move you made
was to dip me,
my hair flying back,
laughter bubbling from my lungs.

I suppose it was then that I knew,
no other man had ever done it right.

No other man until you.

I searched for you,
and found you,
    in every thankful word I wrote.

The mountains, the river, the sun's golden hue,
and still,
my eyes,
just wouldn't leave you.

My heart feels like it is being
 held very gently,
as we lay here

and watch each other breathe.

She wanted his skin
to just soak into hers.

As steady as the breeze ripples the sea,
I know you will be there,
waiting for me,
with a handful of flowers,
along with that thing,
that smile you have,
that compels me to sing.

THIS IS FOR YOU.

It comes easily,
every moment of my life,
thinking about you.

You are more to me than a smile every morning
and a kiss before good night.
You are my everything I ever dreamed.
You are every good thing in sight.

THIS IS FOR YOU.

I just want you to know,
that I could be your safe place to go.

She liked the messages his eyes were sending.
So she maintained contact
　　until a bridge formed between them.

They had that good,
old-fashioned kind of love.
The humble kind.
The kind that speaks for itself.

Life -

It was everything I wanted,
before I knew
that I wanted you.

To tell him to stop calling me beautiful is pointless.
He says it too often.
"But darling,
to withhold truth is to lie."
And with that,
he had me silent.

When there is no one there to remind you of happiness,
        look back on those sweet moments,
when he stroked your hair
and stared into your eyes with earnest,
when he shyly glanced down to your lips
and blushed as he redirected his gaze,
when he slid his hands down your arms and into your hold.
He leans forward, nose to nose, and gently, kindly,
touches his lips to yours.

Exhale.

What makes you think that I love you?
Is it the way my eyes look into yours?
The way my hand reaches for your fingers?
The way my heart touches your strings?

Because if that is the way,
then you have finally seen me.

His tongue was an ointment,
        forming words that caressed her heart
with gentleness.
As a stream over blistered toes.

THIS IS FOR YOU.

You keep trickling into my memory,
like a stream meeting the sea,
my own personal estuary
of just you and me.

She watched the grass move from side to side,
    the wind gently grazing its edges.
"That's how I'd like to be held," she thought.
Firmly enough to be moved,
    but gently enough to look forward to the touch.

Is he tall?
Oh, he is over 6 feet tall.
But does his character match?

It kissed you
how I wanted to,
the sun meeting your skin.

THIS IS FOR YOU.

I could never forget about you,
even if I never wrote a word.

She found someone
   who ripped off her mask,
who would not settle for her shell.

THIS IS FOR YOU.

I got caught up in his smile,
and became a tangled,
beautiful mess.

I'm only afraid that you don't know how much I love you.
But I suppose that's a good problem to have.
To love someone so completely that no actions, no words,
    seem to do it any justice.

Her heart was wooden, hard, splintering.
Gentleness was not her suit.
But she met him,
and the wood became wood chips,
washed away by a flowing pool of fresh water,
through which she hoped to fill his soul.

You know what the most beautiful thing is?
That you came back to me because you were healed,
not because you were broken.

He had the kind of touch
that invited her to stay.
His fingers told a story
of a gentler time and place.

She knew, from that first moment
their fingers interlaced,
that he'd been taking care,
of all she'd lost along the way.

When he first spoke,
she quivered with ecstasy.
His voice matched that which she had always dreamed.

Perhaps I would've loved harder and earlier on
if I knew that love like this existed.
But then again,
it must've been meant to be,
that it would wind up,
just you and me.

There is no ulterior motive here.
My heart is simply yours.

They wanted to know
what my favorite feature about him was.
The question confused me.
I studied his face and could only think,
to choose one feature
was to discriminate against the rest.
"But I love the whole thing,"
I said with a whisper.

You have found the one
      when he tells you that everything about you is
beautiful,
      and you believe him.

THIS IS FOR YOU.

I feel happy
just imagining being in your arms.

Every word you spoke
felt like home.
You were the most familiar new thing
I'd ever known.

You taught me that love is simpler
than the world would like us to think.

You and me. This is simplicity.

"Eyes are the window to the soul," they say.
And his are the kindest I've ever seen.

He was my dreams
come to life in a man.

He gently removed her thorns
until all that was left
was the sweetness of the rose.

You are rare.
You stand out in a crowd.
You drive him wild.
And he will not leave you more beautiful
    than he found you.
Because he will not leave you.

Marriage -

They loved because they chose.
And that was the most romantic thing I'd ever seen.

He loved her,
and she loved him.
And together they taught each other
how to love themselves the same.

When he looked into her eyes,
he looked into an entryway.
She invited him into her home,
and she invited him to stay.

She was a breath of mountain air
in a city full of smog.

THIS IS FOR YOU.

The crease on his hand
looked a whole lot to her like the road home.

Trace the edges of my face
because darling, that is all it takes,
    to fall in love again.

Love.
It exists.
And I'm sorry if you've been made to question that.

It's simple to me.
Falling in love with you,
over and over,
each day.

Whatever you're doing,
you're doing it well.
Keep existing,
and I promise,
I'll stay.

THIS IS FOR YOU.

You are my human journal.

"You are so beautiful," he said.
"The way your hair falls,
        and the way your face exists."

He couldn't hide the love in his eyes.
But then again,
she was certain,
he hardly tried.

I love you in the days
we haven't yet seen.

Chapter 2: Part II - The next hello.

When you're away,
I write,
until I'm almost sure
I feel your skin
brush up against mine.

It's called preemptive sadness,
missing you before you're gone.

Greatest fear -

I've grown weary of being apart from you,
and you have not yet left.
As if the mere thought of it exhausts my soul.

She was sure that just hearing his voice
would add years to her life.

"Distance makes the heart grow fonder"
Yes.
But it also makes the heart grow faint.
Day by day, fatigue sets in.
Pain is tiring.
But even when the pain stays,
when it grows,
when your whole body aches with exhaustion,
when you don't think you can survive one more day
without an embrace from the one you love,
remember that pain will one day turn to sweetness.
You will hurt,
and you will cry,
but my dear, you are strong.
And your God is stronger still.

I long to tell you something,
but I don't know what to say or how to say it.
I don't even really know what it is I feel.
I know that I miss you,
 but that is not it.
I know that I love you,
 but neither is it that.
Language is putting limitations on my soul.

Perhaps what I long to say cannot be said
but must be touched.
I long to be with you, my dear.
And when I am with you,
 you will understand the language of my soul.

My touch will speak to you.
My eyes will translate its message.
There will be nothing lost and no more longing
trapped within me,
 for it will be freed upon you.

It was in those deepest moments
of missing him
that she wished she could hold
her own heart in her hands
to be sure it would stay together.

There were few things going on in her mind,
aside from how much she hurt for his presence
and how much his absence left her heavy inside.

As soon as she said goodbye,
she was aching
for the next hello.

A homecoming - (pgs. 112 - 113)

(1/2) He pressed his nose against the glass,
cupping his eyes with his hands.

I was there,
sitting calmly in my chair,
a book in hand,
a cup of coffee on the stand.

A smile teased the crease of his lips.
He knocked a silly rhythm.
I glanced up and saw him,
peeking into my world.

What joy in that moment,
flooded his face,
flooded mine.

Here we were,
apart for so long,
to now reunite.

And it was then that I knew,
the most heart-swelling,
cheesy, we-were-meant-to-be songs,

(2/2) were not inspired by those moments of
"I missed you."
But by the thrilling present tense of,
"I no longer have to."

For the friend who lost someone -

She often sits back
and listens for your voice.
And sometimes she's sure she can hear it,
rumbling deep, comforting,
making the most missed, familiar noise.

You linger with her.
You always will, I believe.
And she's thankful that you linger
because your lingering on her
means she can linger on you too.

And most days,
that is simply all she wants to do.

But she thanks God,
that she can rest here.
She can rest here and know,
that one day,
she'll be exclaiming the most joyous *"hello"*.

Heaven is for you.

You are too pure for death to touch you.
You did not die, so much as you simply found your home
in a place more beautiful and fitting for your soul.

And though you are gone,
your actions still sing
a gentle hymn of peace.

THIS IS FOR YOU.

You are alive in me,
through old, sweet memory.

Chapter 3 - Cracked pots.

Your story matters to someone.
You just need to speak it.

This is my testimony - (pgs. 119 - 120)

(1/2) My story was not so special.
I grew up well,
in a warm home
with warm friends,
and a warm family.

Where my story got special
was where the darkness came into play,
where the light battled the evil,
where sin ventured out of its cave.

The battle was vicious.
It was not won with ease.
There was blood, ripped hearts,
many broken seams.

What you did not see,
you on the outskirts,
was the story in my mind,
the plot that thickened with every sunrise.

(2/2) As hard as I tried,
my fighting was weak.
I grasped for more strength,
but quickly learned of defeat.

But my story is memorable,
and I will tell you just why.
I won a war, you see,
with nothing more than a cry.

A silent cry out for help,
for some mercy to find
this frail child of God
simply desperate to survive.

I am here still, you see,
because the Lord heard my plea
and mercifully, He set me
absolutely free.

You're a fool
if you think she is weaker for her brokenness.
The hard things didn't ruin her.
Before, she was a shell,
void of experience,
void of understanding,
empathy,
wisdom.
Her broken points are strong now.
She is full.

Vulgarity -

As a woman, I demand respect.
I am not invisible.
I am here.

When you make your vulgar,
sexual,
demeaning jokes,

know that I am here.

I must forgive myself for worrying about
how I am supposed to react,
not wanting to be thought of as obnoxious.

That is not my problem.
You are my problem.

To set the record straight,
Calling a woman beautiful is not degrading *when spoken
through understanding lips.*
Beautiful means so many different things.
It is physical.
But more so, a woman becomes beautiful
because of her inner being that seeps out of her skin.
If you can't see that,
if you do not believe in the positivity of beauty,
of being called beautiful,
then you are missing such a sweet piece of being.
Of loving.
Of seeing.
Of feeling.
"You are beautiful" is precious.
"You are beautiful" is hardly profanity.

Regret -

It hit me hard,
when I said goodbye to you,
that this may be our last memory.
And that, if it was,
I would be ashamed.
I had been acting out of such selfishness to you.
Forgive me from afar.
So that I know, that you know, that I love you too.

Kneeling,
tears,
hands clasped.

It's been too long
since standing,
but my soul needs this rest on the ground.

I am only breathing because I am here.

I leapt forward.
The world let me fall
through the floor,
crashing,
hurdling,
breaking bones,
my heart.

And I had no will to even scream.

We wear masks to
please other people,
when all people want to see
is a real face.

And this is how relationships starve.

Homesick -

She lay there,
staring at the clock
Tick tick tick
The pendulum swayed
but mostly in her mind.

She becomes a different person
when she's alone,
and she hasn't decided
which person is home.

I gave you my opinion,
    and you gave me back the brutal fact,
that you were not prepared to listen.

You have never been hard to love.
They were just never very good at loving.

The contradiction of tears -

Amazing, how tears are so silent
while pain is so loud.

Grief is not fleeting.
It hovers.
Burns.
Reminds.
But year after year, finger by finger,
it will let your windpipe go,
until it is only a faint pressure,
like something always checking for a pulse,
reminding you now that you are still alive.

This is not a dream -

You see me from the outside.
You see a dream.
Step into my optics,
and see what I see.
Feel what I feel,
and you will know that dream worlds
do not exist here.

Explain depression -

Well,
that is the struggle;
isn't it?

It is all at once
or none at all,
an emptiness
that is much too full.

She was the epitome of intellect leading to ruin.
She was the overthinking goddess turned shriveled
and disillusioned child.
She was the master of nothing,
     salivating to be the master of all.
Her brain was a deadly weapon used against her.

Be careful when you criticize,
when you tell someone to
"bloom where they are planted".
You have no idea whether they were planted near sunshine.

A flower can only do so much.

She did not promise she would be easy -

You,
you know she needs you,
but please do not make her beg;
do not dare make her grovel.
She has done so much already.
She has done so much to make sure you know
that she loves you.

So when she is dark,
when she is not responding how you would like her to,
know that she needs you,
but that she is hoping all that saved up memory will do.

Her worst fear
was for anyone to think she was stone-cold,
when really,
her heart was shattering,
her soul crying out.

Her eyes stayed dry;
her voice stayed even.
Consider it her curse.

It's ok to be sad.
And it's ok to let that sadness overcome you.
People who tell you otherwise understand sadness
by a smaller definition.

But dear,
do not let grief overcome you for too long.
It does not deserve such power.
Strike it down with moments of joy.
Kill it with thanksgiving.

She is made up of painful opinions
that bite through her skin
and lash out of her mouth like a whip.
Justified opinions but ones that some don't want to hear
because to them
she is fire.
Out of control and wild.
Out of her boundaries.
A woman who thinks.
Her thoughts burn their skin,
tear into their flesh,
pull out their lashes.
But to those who understand,
her words are like lotion,
soothing to the ears and cool to the touch.
Her femininity mixed with opinion is too much for some
and perfectly wonderful for those who are, themselves,
lovers of thought that contradicts their own.

She wondered
how many stones they would have to throw at her,
    before they saw that she was right.

The cruel words poured out of her throat.
And just like that,
she broke another human.
And when you break another human,
you break a little too.

Real men are tired of being told they are not.

"Why do you believe in something that is so hard?"
He said with frustration.
She looked at him with deep, convicted eyes,
"Just because it's hard doesn't mean it's not True."

He was silent.

I am aware,
that the smile on your face
does not match the fog in your eyes.

I know there's more to you than that shell you show.
The shell is intricate;
it is beautiful; I'm sure you know.
But shells usually hide something within,
something alive that is trying to grow.

I'm starting to learn
   that when people say they're tired,
more often than not,
   they mean that their soul is weary.

THIS IS FOR YOU.

The problem wasn't that they were searching for
worth in the wrong places.
The problem was that they were searching for
something they already had.

The only ridiculous dreams
are the ones you have no intention of pursuing.

We all just need to hear:
"You are welcome in this heart;
you are welcome in this life."

You'll make a difference in someone's life,
    whether you want to or not.
The choice you have
is what type of difference that will be.

And whether you'll be proud to think,
"Oh yes, that quality, that one came from me."

I believe you are better than this,
even if you believe that you are not.

You're yelling so loudly that all they hear is noise.
Talk gently, my dear.
Maintain your poise.

Perhaps we hear God's voice the loudest
when we grow tired of
screaming and grasping,
when we finally go completely

silent.

Depression & Body - (pgs. 156 - 159)

(1/4) It buries into my chest, twisting and lodging,
indulging in flesh.
I scream in scalding silence, resisting the pain,
effort, I soon learn, expended entirely in vain.

I suffocate, gasp for air,
suffer in lonely solitude and despair.
I scramble for light, for some semblance of right,
for some chance that this is simply temporary.

But it engulfs me.
I scream, and I claw at the ground.
God SAVE ME! Where have You gone from me now?!
I am sick. I am tired. I am supposedly Your child?!
So why am I here?
With bloody fingernails, lying half dead on the ground?

I imagine You watching me.
You selfish King. You wretched Being who thrives off the
pleas of your suffering creations.
This is not Love. This is not Truth. This is not Hope.

God, I do not WANT You.

(2/4) If I was as selfish as You I'd be gone from this pain.
I'd be free from this torture.
I would be done with this game.

I fall deeper into the pit.
My hands thrashed to pieces,
as I punch at the walls.
My feet turn to dust, as I stumble and fall.
My heart turns to ash, and my soul violently frays.
But one drop of water on my cheek stays.

I lay there, salt crusting around the drop.
And I hear something coming down from the top.
"I am here!" the voice says.
"Listen to me now!" it commands.

"SHUT UP!" I scream back,
"I don't believe it is You."

"Child LISTEN; I promise it is True."

"But where have you BEEN?"
I scream through the sobs.
"I don't understand You, no, not at all."

(3/4) "Beloved, you must listen.
I will always love you, but you chose to let the world be
your teacher.

It taught you to hate. To hate yourself.
To love the way she is but to hate the way you are.
You look at yourself and see the world.
See Me! See Me, beloved!

The world promises affirmation if you're thin,
if your skin is perfection,
and your hair is all pinned.
If you adhere to its rules,
you'll have happiness, love, marriage, a pension,

but child, let Me tell you, the world will leave you in
tension.

There is nothing wrong with being thin.
Nothing wrong with being pinned,
but why
do you struggle and cry
for something I am telling you is all a big lie?"

My face dropped, too ashamed to open my eyes.
The single drop of salt fell from my face.

(4/4) He reached down, lifting my chin to His gaze.
"Child, you are healed."

And for the first time in years,
I looked in the mirror and didn't hate what I saw.

The God of the universe had said, "I am in awe."

What an amazing thing,
when she realized that her body
was not meant to be viewed in pieces.

We're all visionaries.
It's just that some of us close our eyes,
when we should keep them open.

Have you ever just looked at another human
and thought that it is impossible for him, or for her,
to not have a Designer,
that there is no way something so beautiful
could exist on its own?

This is what I think when I look at you.

My dear, you aren't just any piece of art.
You are a masterpiece,
designed with no comparison in mind.

The pages of her journal
gave the best advice.

How comforting it would be
if we could wrap our souls in blankets too.

As faith grows - (pgs. 165 - 166)

(1/2) Remember when you were four,
and your dad asked you to jump off that rock
into the water?
And you jumped because he was there below you
with his arms open wide.
You knew he'd catch you and pull you up
before you sank.
I think that's what God asks us to do sometimes.
He asks us to jump
when it doesn't make sense to us.
He asks us to venture into uncharted territory
where we feel out of place and unnatural.
And we often doubt that He is there,
waiting for us with His arms open wide,
ready to catch us before we sink.
And once we jump,
once we realize that God has caught us yet again,
we are quicker to trust,
quicker to jump.
With every "Yes, Lord, I will jump," our anxieties lessen
and become almost a silly thing next to the Almighty power
of our God.
The fear so often associated with an unknown future is
drowned out by hope laden praises.

(2/2) Glory to God,
Who asks us to jump
and Who pulls us to the surface when we do.

Mornings are so peaceful;
the day is still clean.

Maybe, one day,
    all that time that vanished will come back,
and we'll know much better
    what to do with it.

What you cannot imagine
being able to do;
do it.

It will help you imagine it better.

I pray,
that we would have the courage, strength, and love
to not crumble,
but to rise above.

The words stuck to her throat,
and instead of drinking water,

she poured down more honey.

Because part of her knew,
those words were never supposed to
make her money.

Part I - Control

She knew,
from the very start,
that the words he spoke
did not reflect his heart.

Oh yes, she was sure.
His was a soul
that held onto far too much control.

Part II - Free

He had much more depth
than he let others see,
until one day he woke up
and decided
to be free.

You helped me carry
what I could not carry on my own.
You didn't think anything of it,
but I want you to know
that you were the only one who was kind
simply because you wanted to be,
not for a show.

I read the words
and sighed.
This was my heart on a page.

She is the good kind of wild.

The kind that feeds energy into other people,
that makes the ordinary feel magnificent,
the wild that everyone hopes to find,
and that those who do,
never dream of letting go.
Because they know,
that this wild
is the good kind.

She reached out her fingertips
   and touched her future.

And she smiled
because it was soft and warm
   and filled with color.

She breathed life into people,
simply,
by showing appreciation the moment she felt it.

The creature beneath her had no idea
that she was guiding it to a beautiful place.

It just galloped on,
no care for time or space,
purely just enjoying
the joy of the race.

What an absolutely lovely way to live.

In her, hope is an always enduring thing.
It is in itself a purpose,
existing in every moment, in all time, in all space.

How powerful it is,
to trust like that,
to trust that *there is not one thing,*
that hope can not resuscitate.

She stepped into the maze.
There were so many ways.
But the solution is simple.
Start walking, and pray.

Some people are like a good book,
hard to understand at first,
but as time goes on,
impossible to put down.

Her eyes spoke peace and kindness,
and her smile was the undeniable,
contagious action.

It was when she stopped viewing herself
as an object meant to be beautiful
that she finally felt how she had always imagined
it would feel if she were just that.

Beautiful.

With this new day,
I hope you know,
that you, dear one, are meant to grow.
You are meant to be challenged.
You will sometimes get stuck.

And when you do,
we're meant to help each other up.

When your desires,
your cravings,
your drives for life are so
entirely divergent
from what is accepted by the world,
this is how you know
you are doing something right.

Our bodies are not created to be passed around carelessly.

She never rose to the occasion.
Because dear, she was the occasion
for which everyone else had to rise.

Hope -

Here is a word to quench your thirst
to water what is parched
to nourish what hurts.

She was a field of wildflowers,
effortlessly spreading her beauty
into all the thistles and weeds.

They held hands tightly, leaving no room for fear.

Her feet took her far
from all that she knew,
yet with each step she took,
her faith only grew.

She knew there was more
than what she saw in clear sight,
so she drew her strength
from the One with infinite might.

So many of us,
    when we're searching for our permanent resting place,
are searching for a person,
    rather than a space.

For some people,
you will be too strong,
even though you are doing exactly
what you are meant to do.

You are just like the sun.

She dipped her toes into the gentle stream
and was taken back to the days
when she ran through the forest with sticks,
exploring a world that didn't even exist.

It was that type of imagining,
that type of dreaming,
that she hoped every child of hers would have,
the opportunity to explore and invent,
create and find joy,
in things not seen by those around them.

THIS IS FOR YOU.

You have always been quite beautiful,
even before you were told it was so.

How poetic,
that her natural reaction was to be kind.

We were not made to play victim.
We were made to endure, rise up, and defeat.

But have you considered, dear,
that dreams don't die of natural causes?

THIS IS FOR YOU.

Settlers -

They dug into her soul and settled as friends.

Then there was that day,
when I tried to summit a peak but was forced to turn back.
Even so,
    the attempt was the most amazing thing I'd ever done.

The rolling hills were a sea full of green,
a place she thought might make her feel free.
Yet she knew that freedom wasn't so much a place
but was rather the mindset to give herself grace.

She decided to walk into the unknown,
into a place she had yet to call home.

A forest of tattoos,
she saw them all stare.
She smirked…

"Keep staring,
and they'll stick to you too.
Oh, and trust me,
not one of these pieces
was meant to please you."

If someone proves you wrong,
it's ok to be thankful.

It's one of those nights
when the only option
is to write.

I'm not afraid of change.
My whole life has been change,
and I much prefer who I am now
to who I was then.

She spilled her ink all over the page,
but what formed wasn't messy,
it was her art uncaged.
When she looked down, she thought,
"What a lovely display,
of how something so beautiful
came from a mistake."

Re-purposed -

The leaves fell softly from the tree.
Rich, golden, yellows and oranges.
Their time had come to move on from the branches
even though they'd made a home there for so long.
And now, they make the sidewalks streets of gold.

THIS IS FOR YOU.

Small Town -

Clean.
Pure.
Natural.
Quiet.
Birds are the loudest characters you'll find here.

You are broken.
But so am I.
And that is why I love humankind.
We are all so broken,
but we are also still alive.

Thankful -

Be thankful for a beautiful day,
for the jacket that keeps you warm,
and the kids who keep you laughing,
for singing random songs,
and eating raw brownie batter,

for doing your best.

Be like a sunflower,
a marigold,
a poppy, my dear.
    Always turn towards the light.

Know that if you ever need a hand to hold,
I will empty mine for you.

There was a light in her eyes,
a hint of the colorful spirit within.

The blankest of pages,
the blankest of lives,
she brightened with a single try.

This was her artistic gift.

Why are you fighting so hard to stay relevant?
You are a human being.
You will always be relevant to me.

Sometimes
it's ok to run,
not away from the pain,
but towards the freedom.

And I truly don't care how far away you run,
so long as you save some energy
to come home.

She did not try to prove herself.
She just let herself be.
And her being
was all the worth she needed.

How freeing.

A picture paints a thousand words,
and a few words mean a thousand more.

I am a woman.
And it does not make me feel weak.
I give birth.
I nurture.
I grow life.
I sacrifice.
How is it that any woman allows inferiority
to be her complex?
We are anything but.
We are powerhouses.
We are strength.
We are beauty.

Darling, there is no shame
      in loving the sun freckles on your chest,
in adoring the stretch marks on your hips.
The uniqueness is yours.
The abnormality,
   your design.

THIS IS FOR YOU.

Tell me,
why is it that I can not tell your passion
by looking at your life?

She let the wind blow through her hair,
as she let the past unwind its snare.

She found joy in places where the world said,
"You can't have that here."
But she held onto it.

And suddenly, darkness felt fear.

Nature -

Sweet friend, I think you need
to brew some coffee in the mountains,
to sit awhile with no responsibility
but to listen to the wind.
You'll find your way.

Dreams - (pgs. 225 - 226)

(1/2) There was a field of grass.
I looked at all the thousands of blades.
Each one represented a dream,
standing firm, individual but together.

But then a shadow passed over the blades;
a boot came down and crushed them.

I cried for awhile,
thinking about how those blades of grass
had no idea what was coming for them.

They were doing so well,
growing roots into rich soil,
and all it took was a shoe to crumple them,
to take away all that hard work.

A couple days later, I went back to that spot.
Those blades,
they were standing up again.

It was incredible,
the way they looked sturdy still,
like nothing had ever harmed them.

(2/2) There was a brown mark on one of them,
a crease on another,
but it made them look more wild,
more capable of survival in the real world.

"My dreams will make it," I thought.
They are not useless to me yet.

Cling to the pureness of your soul;
good is still fighting.
And I promise you,
good wins.

She exhaled, as He whispered in her ear,
"I am here. I am here."

Every scar on this skin
lets me know that this place
will stay with me forever,
through scraped knees and grace.

I have never seen anything more comforting
than flowers growing out of a cracked pot.

It's strange,
how I often feel joy and pain
should not be mixed in a story,
as if those two things can only be found
in separate places.

The sun is out,
so I let it kiss my skin
to remind me how it feels
to let the warmth back in.

Hope reminds us
that darkness wasn't made to last.

Her soul felt heavier
   than it needed to feel.
So she stepped back, took time,
   and let herself heal.

She broke completely.
And when she did,
all the grime spilled out

and left her clean.

We can love so many people,
so deeply,
without reaching our end.
But the moment we feel hatred for one person,
our energy is spent.
This should tell us all we need to know about our hearts
and their purpose.
This should remind us to stay true,
to what our hearts are meant to do.

THIS IS FOR YOU.

Her heart was
Frightening.
Mysterious.
Beautiful.

A wilderness made to last.

If you are real,
let me feel your flaws,
even if it hurts.

THIS IS FOR YOU.

Your joy waters my wilting heart.

She didn't realize how much power words had
until she was destroyed by them,
and then until she was so loved by them
that she forgot she was ever destroyed.

When it is hard -

For days, I prayed that I would no longer be the outsider,
that I would feel comfortable
so I could focus on being a light.
But then I realized that being a light
in a place where everyone is trying to put you out
creates a more noticeable flame.

So I welcomed the buckets of water,
the attempts at quelling my fire.
And eventually, they couldn't help but realize,
that my light did not need to be accepted to be seen.

I counted You as a fraud,
but then You dug the dirt out from over me;
You grabbed my hand and dragged me to the surface
and told me that You saved me because
You heard me cry out from under the ground.

THIS IS FOR YOU.

Challenge -

I am beginning to see the beauty of this challenge.
I am beginning to see you.

Go -

Go where the light is,
and stay there forever.

Wherever you feel most whole,
go to that place.

But do not forget about those
who have not yet found the light.

Remember them.
Because to forget
would mean to withhold the light for yourself,
and that is not its purpose.

Light spreads.

Your weakness does not repel God.

Psalms -

How humbling,
every morning,
to be reminded that the greatest poetry
has already been written.

THIS IS FOR YOU.

Let the brightest light,
come from the depths of your soul.
Illuminate us.

You don't need a key.
She leaves her heart unlocked,
welcoming you to see.

Lean into me and trust,
for as long as you stay,
I will not step away.

When we met, You killed something in me.
You killed the darkness,
something I did not even think You could see.

And now I sit here, thinking of You.
Thinking how, through death, You gave me life,
through death, You made me free,

and how maybe some deaths aren't as bad
as they're chalked up to be.

She mined for the gold in people,
even when the risk was high,
and found it to be worthwhile,
every single time.

What do I think?
I think poetry could never do you justice.
But it is beautiful nonetheless.
So then, what must that say about you?

And I knew that it was finished,
when the words
no longer kept me up at night.

The End.

65374678R00161

Made in the USA
San Bernardino, CA
02 January 2018